the **best** *in*

lingerie

design

the **best** *in*
lingerie
design

Joy McKenzie

◄ **Playtex:** 'Wonderbra' in iris.
44 fabric pieces and 25 stitching
processes are employed for the
push-up and plunge effect.

Acknowledgements

I would like to thank my family and friends, and also those most directly involved in the production of this publication without whose support it would not have been possible. To Richard Reynolds, Martina Stansbie and Julie Ambrose at B.T. Batsford Ltd; Janet and Eliza Reger of Janet Reger Ltd; June Kenton of Rigby & Peller Ltd; Jeremy Farrell; Rosemary Hawthorn; Helen Stanley; John Hammond and Monica Fernandez of R.D. Franks; Helen Taylor, Associate Fashion Editor for *Fashion Weekly*; Laurian Davies, Publicity Executive for Womenswear at the British Knitting and Export Council; Sue Hall, Advertising Director of Underlines; Annie Jones, Advertising and Sales Manager for *Lingerie Buyer*; Bill Hook, editor of *Bodystyle Magazine*; Martin Short, Senior Classified Consultant for *Fashion Index*, EMAP Fashion Ltd., Sara Hyams, Manageress for the Lingerie Department at Harrods; Willie Beuth, Managing Director of Ecotex; the London College of Fashion Library; Victoria and Albert Museum; National Art Library; The British Retail Consortium and the British Fashion Council.

Dedication

This book is dedicated to my parents, Mitchell and Monica McKenzie.

Printed in China
for the Publisher
B.T. Batsford Ltd
583 Fulham Road
London SW6 5BY

ISBN 0 7134 8028 9

A CIP catalogue record for this book is available from the British Library.

contents

Foreword   6

Introduction   8

Brassieres   10

Camisoles, vests and bodies   46

Corsetry   68

Nightwear   82

Panties   96

Petticoats and slips   120

Index   124

Foreword

Janet Reger

I have dedicated most of my life to capturing the essence of feminine beauty, combined it with the spirit of love and romance, added a generous measure of glamour and created the intoxicating cocktail of seduction and sensuality that has become my personal hallmark for luxurious lingerie.

◀ **Janet Reger:** mini slip in pure silk satin with appliqued lace.

Introduction

'Without foundation there can be no fashion.'
Christian Dior (1905–57)

Lingerie has always been determined by the silhouettes demanded by fashion, but equally important has been a revolution in the manufacture of fabrics over the last 50 years. The rationing of the Second World War and the corresponding shortage of cotton and silk was followed by the mass manufacture of artificial fibres in the 1950s. Nylon, non-absorbent but porous in weave, was widely used up until the 1970s and Lycra, the most important of a range of man-made elastics called elastomeric fibres or elastane, first became available in 1959. Lighter yet more powerful than rubber, Lycra became prevalent during the 1980s, and together with stretch lace, knitted simplex, nylon, cotton polyester, 'climatic' fibres (which protect the wearer from intemperate conditions) and other elastic fabrics, has brought about new possibilities in design.

Today the trend in fashion tends to place an emphasis on health, comfort and fit. Women no longer conceal their bodies under layers of foundation garments or cage themselves in tightly-laced corsets. Lycra's smooth stretch properties reflect the influence of sportswear and, in turn, influence leisurewear. Footless tights, leggings, leotards, cropped tops and bodies are usually manufactured from a cotton/Lycra mix, and are worn as everyday wear by the vast majority of young women.

From the 1820s to the 1990s lingerie has been finding its way to the surface, with corset-shaped tops notable for crossing the boundary between underwear and outerwear. Madonna's corset of 1990, designed by Jean Paul Gaultier, was inspired by the 'whirlpool' spirals of the bras of the 1950s.

The Best in Lingerie Design will be glancing at lingerie's historical context before concentrating on the designs themselves. Today there is something for every woman: from separates to matching sets, from camisoles, slips and knickers to cropped tops and tangas. It is this richness and variety of design - in colour, shape, form and line - which forms the focus of this book.

◀ **Gossard:** 'Gypsy' in red.

Brassieres

The bra has compressed, enlarged and pushed the bust up and down according to the fashion of the day. Early terms such as 'bust extender', 'bust shaper', 'bust bodice' and 'bust flattener' defined the bra's shape, and, to an extent, reflected the concerns of its wearer. As women of the 1920s demonstrated their emancipation, fashion followed with the 'boyish look' and a demand for underwear that flattened the bust. By contrast, brassieres of the 1950s, when fashion's emphasis was on femininity, gave the bust a lift with circular or whirlpool stitching that created a cone-like effect, and made the bust fuller with foam pads known as 'falsies' and 'cuties'.

It was not until the 1930s that brassieres were designed with distinct, shaped cups to separate, enhance and support the breasts. By the following decade, cup size had become as important in fitting as all-round bust measurements. Fitting was increasingly refined after the Second World War with the development of 'AA' to 'FF' sizes, and a 'G' available from specialist companies. However, despite the even greater range available today and the presence of a consultant in most department stores and lingerie boutiques, 70 to 85 per cent of women still wear a bra of the wrong size.

In the 1940s and 1950s, popular bras had long lines and hook-and-eye front fastenings, while the 1960s saw many low-cut styles with wide straps and even a 'No-Bra-Bra' (1969), suitable for women who did not have the nerve fully to embrace the bra-less look. The increasing use of stretch fabrics saw pants and bras moulded seamlessly from one piece of elastane, while bras emulated bikini tops with triangular rather than rounded cups, and were made from jersey, transparent or matt fabrics, with little or no padding.

By the 1980s 'cami-vests' and 'cami-tops' provided a bra-less look, a forerunner of the 1990s' sports bras. Due to developments in fabric manufacture, the prevalence of lycra and ever more advanced design techniques, the range now available is vast, from backless and strapless styles to sports bras, cropped tops and cleavage inducing bras.

▶ **La Perla:** 'Sculpture' Note the ultra-flat centre seam which applies an appropriate tension to the fabric of the cup for a close fit.

▲ Gottex:

'Fashion' padded and underwired plunge
bra kept sleekly simple with clever boning
and seaming.

▶ **Gottex:** 'Opera' padded and
underwired bra with tanga brief.

◀ **Warners:** 'Pure Luxury' balconette bra in vibrant sugar pink from a sheer microfibre embroidered with polka dots and trimmed with fine Swiss embroideries.

▼ **Warners:** 'Odyssey' padded bustier in black from a delicately embossed satin Lycra trimmed with soft textured Calais lace.

▲ **Donna Karan:** 'Secrets' cream
Lace with Lycra bra and pants worn
with lilac jacquard acetate/rayon with
Lycra blouse by Rifat Ozbek - the
ultimate in luxurious lingerie and fabrics.

▼ **Rosy:** Lace with Lycra bra and pants. Soft blue-on-blue two-tone lace for a new take on the beauty of traditional lace lingerie.

▲ **Lejaby:** 'Candide' bra and knickers
in embroidered jersey. Undercups of
soft and supple broderie anglais jersey
complement straps of festooned ribbon
while open thread work highlights the
edges of bra and knickers.

▶ **Lejaby:** 'Nuage' bra and knickers.
Smoothness under clothes is
guaranteed by the seamless cups of the
bra. Note the attractive contrast
between the matt and shiny skin-soft
microfibre/Lycra fabric.

▼ Laetitia Allen:
'Moonflower' underwired bra.

▲ **La Senza:** 'Body Sculptures'
underwired and seam free bra.

▶ **Silhouette:** backless bra.

Silhouette

▼ **Silhouette:** strapless bra.

◀ **Eda:** bra with preformed cups in chiffon and satin.

▼ **Eda:** bra and brief set from the Leavers Lace range.

▼ **La Perla:** 'Plisse' in black. Intricate pleating makes this bra a fashion winner in its own right.

▲ **La Perla:** 'Rondo', low-cut,
underwired and heavily edged in lace.

◀ **Warners:** 'Muse'
balconette bra and brief set in ink blue.

▲ **Warners:** 'Simply Sensational' bustier and brief in tricotronic jacquard and 2-way stretch Lycra with Swiss guipure embroidery.

◄ **Playtex:** 'Wonderbra'in champagne. Wonderbra's original gate-back and full power netting ensures that the bra cups stay in place to maintain maximum cleavage.

▲ **La Perla:** 'Etoile'

▼ **Lovable Italiana:** 'Ambra' push up bra. Raised embroidery is effective for a textured look: large marguerite daisies combine with highly tactile matt Lycra charmeuse and striking colour.

▲ **Lovable:** 'Lov'Concept' underwired bra.
A floating element seamed inside the bra gives support that
is invisible yet secure. High-performance Tactel Aquator
fabric allows perspiration to evaporate, keeping the skin
completely dry. Soft and light, the fabric is teamed with an
embroidered-effect lace for an attractive and sleek look.

▲ **Gossard:** 'Ultrabra' in sea-spray
Lace with Lycra. A classic design
updated by the latest colours and Lycra
technology. Worn with a checked
cotton with Lycra skirt by Joseph.

▼ **Cacharel:** rose Lace with Lycra padded bra; Capucine Puerari peach-pink net Lace with Lycra 50s knickers.

▼ **Valisere:** 'Seine' bustier.
Embroidered flowers on cotton crepe
combine with broderie anglaise.

▶ **Jane Woolrich** 'Fleur de Lys' bra
and matching thong in silk satin with
heavily textured embroidered lace. The
design takes its inspiration from the
sensuousness of the lace pattern.

▲ **La Senza:** jacquard bra and brief set.

▼ Exotica: Knickers from Brazil:
Underwired bra and matching Brazilian
knickers in satin and lace trim with Lycra.
The half cup underwired bra is perfect for
wearing with low-cut styles.

◀ **Exquisite Form:** 'Ful-ly 505 'X'quisite comfort' bra.
An underarm 'X' seam replaces the conventional vertical seam and provides a self-adjusting pivotal point for perfect fit. The top and bottom parts of the 'X' adjust to movement independently, preventing the bra slipping or riding up.

▲ **Felina:** bra and brief set.

▶ **Damart:** Racer back sports bra,
▼ from a nylon/elastane/cotton mix.
The racer back gives the ease of
movement needed for exercise while
seam free cups cut down on friction.

▶ **Patricia of Finland:** Sports bra
in coolmax Lycra and cotton with
matching brief.

▲ **Triumph:** Tri-Action 2001. The broad underbust band prevents the bra riding up during exercise while seamless cups, graded slightly smaller and cut higher than a normal bra, press the bust gently but firmly against the body, so eliminating chafing.

▼ **Fila Donna:** front fastening seam free bra with racer back.

▲ **Fila Donna:** sports bra.

Camisoles, vests and bodies

First developed in the mid-nineteenth century, the camisole was designed to be worn over the corset, and was called, somewhat prosaically, a corset cover. The knitted vest was effectively a winter version of the camisole, with both being variants of the long, smock-like chemise.

By the early 1900s, as corsets became lower in design, some form of covering for the breasts was required and camisoles became supplanted by early versions of the bra. The garment was decidedly out of fashion by the 1920s, although its derivatives, 'combinations' such as cami-knickers and cami-petticoats, became extremely popular as their simplicity provided the smooth line required by fashions of the 1920s and 1930s. Another variation of the camisole was the liberty bodice, a soft garment made from fleecy-backed cotton and reinforced with tape. Fastened at the front with bone or rubber buttons with extra buttons around the base to hold up petticoats or suspenders, it was a classic design worn mainly by young girls from 1908 to the 1950s.

Vests developed as a slimmer, briefer version of the chemise and were worn by both men and women. Most usually knitted for warmth, they could also be made from silk or cotton. Combination-style garments were still extremely popular in the 1940s and 1950s, especially combination foundations, incorporating brassiere, girdle, petticoat and knickers, while cami-knickers were slim and elegant and knee-length, their bodices and hems trimmed with nylon lace, pleated nylon tulle or ruffles.

Camisoles and cami-knickers have been adopted for nightwear, though both have been revived in lingerie of the 1990s. The widespread availability of stretch fabrics such as Lycra, and the crossover of sportswear and daywear has led to the proliferation of vest tops and cropped tops, creating a sporty look, as well as the ubiquitous body and the bodyshaper.

▶ **Hanro of Switzerland:** tulle net body with Venetian embroidery: lingerie that blurs the distinction between underwear and outerwear.

◀ **Rigby & Peller:** 'Tuscany'
underwired thong body.

▼ **Rigby & Peller:** 'Ophelia'
underwired body.

Valisere

▼ Valisere: 'Comedie' shoestring strap camisole in gold with embroidered top detail and fluted hem together with matching French knickers.

▲ **Valisere:** 'Capucine' body in white with padded and underwired cups. Stretch net with tiny flocked spots combines with daisy patterned guipure lace for this lightweight body.

▲ **Silhouette:** 'Baroque' body shaper - front view.

▶ **Silhouette:**

'Audace' thong body shaper - for the perfect line under clothes.

▲ **Silhouette:** 'Baroque' body shaper - back view.

◀ **Gottex:** 'Diamond' body suit
with padded cups and stretch
Calais lace trimming detail.

▼ **Gottex:** 'Fashion' body
suit with padded cups and seaming
detail from soft nylon/Lycra fabric.

▼ **Hanro of Switzerland:** 'Velvet Dream' lacy body and bolero jacket.

▲ Hanro of Switzerland:
ribbed sleeveless top and high cut brief.

▲ **Laetitia Allen:** cami top with adjustable shoestring straps and shorts with elasticated waist in jacquard satin.

▶ **Laetitia Allen:** 'Chatelaine' crop top with ruched straps and tanga.

▲ **C&B London:** deep-grey Lace with Lycra vest, shirt and ruched skirt; Wolford 'Fatal' red opaque tights with Lycra.

▼ **Eda:** black and gold jacquardtonic lace body.

▼ **Damart:** rib knit sleeveless vest in a Thermolactyl chlorofibre. This unique lightweight fibre traps warm air next to the body and 'wicks' perspiration to the surface. The closely knitted ribs are soft, stretchy and supple.

▼ **Damart:** Clover-knit French neck vest with delicate
waist trim.

◀ **Malizia by La Perla:** 'Tiffany' in black.

▼ **La Perla:** 'Nain'.

▼ **La Senza:** Spanish daisy romper.

▲ **Warners:** 'Not so Innocent Nudes'
seamless bodyliner.

Corsetry

The 1930s was a momentous period for corsetry design. The development of elastic, available in different gauges for use in lingerie around 1935, meant that corsets became both firmer and lighter, the bulky fabrics from which they were once made banished. Full-length, so as to achieve a smooth line over the hips, these elastic foundation garments bore little resemblance to their forerunners, being increasingly decorative, with varying degrees of control, available in a variety of sizes and fitting the body more accurately with the aid of tight lacing or hooks.

As fabrics became lighter, manufacturers became increasingly concerned with aesthetics, comfort and fit. The latter was particularly important as women's bust, waist and hip measurements vary enormously and the fitting of most corsets had been based on bust or waist measurements only. In 1926, Berlei had pioneered the first ever scientific study into women's proportions, defining five basic figure types into which most women would fall, irrespective of their height or weight. Their system was introduced to the UK in 1930 and other companies followed suit, with Gossard producing a chart defining nine perfect figure types.

By the 1940s, women were encased in a corset which was laced at the back from under the bust to hip level, placing emphasis on the waist. With the outbreak of war, fabric rationing meant less frills and flounces and trimmings such as embroidery and lace. The influence of nylon, invented by Dr Wallace Carother in 1937 and launched by Dupont a year later, was manifested in corsets of the mid-1940s such as the 'Guimpe', 'Guepere' and 'Waspie', designed by couturiers as foundations for the silhouettes of 'The New Look'. Some couture houses began to produce their own lingerie designs or commissioned them so as to provide the perfect foundation for their garments.

The flexibility of girdles and brassieres was increasingly important as women became more physically active, particularly by playing sport. The emphasis of the 1950s was on exercise - a good diet as well as a good corset - and 'National Corset Week' was launched in Britain in 1952. Corsetry became increasingly streamlined with a

▶ **Rigby & Peller:** 'Opera' underwired basque with Brazilian brief.

◀ **Silhouette:** low back basque.

▲ **Ann Summers:** basque.

minimum of seaming, often made from black or white lace and lined with pastel-coloured voile. New designs, such as the 'panty-girdle', helped to eliminate visible panty line (VPL) under tight and clinging garments from jeans to evening gowns.

1960s fashion - fun, short, sweet and very, very brief - was echoed by its corsetry which was firm, strapless or had detachable straps. Girdles became briefer and less rigid, with decorated sections of embroidered nylon, lace, spandex or elastic. The two-way pull style had panels of elastic crossing in an X shape over the stomach and was very popular. By the end of the decade, the long 'corselette' was revived both for day and evening wear.

The lingerie of the 1970s was supple, diminutive and practical, and corsets, girdles and panty girdles became unfashionable, seeming in opposition to the fitness aesthetic of the day.

The 'power dressing' styles of the 1980s saw the return of the corset in a new dual role: as as intimate apparel or as outerwear. Contemporary fashion is still fascinated by body shaping, with designers such as Jean Paul Gaultier, Gianni Versace and Karl Lagerfeld exploring corsetry's shape-giving structures, but today's styles are more decorative than torturous, only evoking memories of the pain and discomfort of Victorian styling.

▼ **Gossard:** white corselet.

▶ **Gossard:** black corselet.

◀ **Silhouette:** 'Chiara' basque with detachable shoulder straps and suspenders.

▼ **Silhouette:** 'Bouquet' smooth basque.

◀ **Jane Woolrich:** 'Fleur de Lys' basque and matching thong in silk satin combined with heavily textured embroidery and front lace-up feature.

▲ **La Perla:** 'Capriccio'.

▶ **Patricia of Finland:** basque in stretch
lace with Lycra and cotton and polyester satin.

▼ **De Pledge:** 'Serenity' basque in
pure silk satin with fine Swiss guipure
lace. The basque is unboned and has
detachable suspenders.

◀ **Damart:** seamless pull-on corset
in elasticated Thermolacyl and Lycra,
providing extra support under the
bust line, at the waist and at the top
of the thighs.

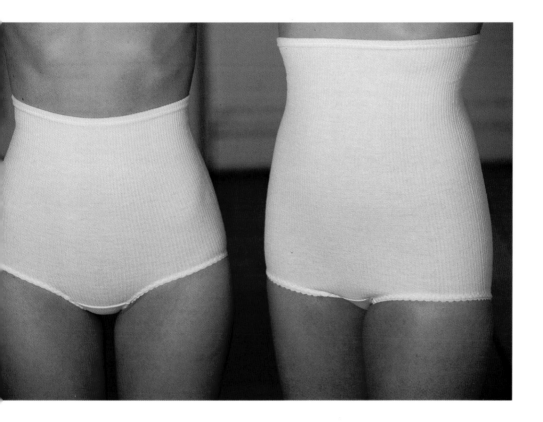

▲ **Damart:** pantie-girdle from
elasticated Thermolactyl and Lycra in
both standard and high-waisted styles.

Nightwear

At the turn of the century, negligees were as luxuriously designed as daywear, with a total disregard for practicality. Like boudoir gowns and tea gowns, they were made from silk and lace, heavily embroidered with gold and silk threads and adorned with jewelled buttons. Bedjackets were frivolous scraps of fabric edged with lace, and oriental kimonos or wrapover gowns with richly quilted cuffs and collars were also worn. Dressing jackets reached to hip level but were soon overtaken in popularity by pyjamas. The latter were available in satins, velvets and lame crepe, first in bright colours, and later in pinks and flesh tones. Many pyjama designs were true to their Persian origin in their colour, print and use of metallic threads and embroidery.

The nightgowns of the 1940s also imitated evening gowns, and were in black georgette or fine silks and satins, with full skirts that reached the mid-calf or even touched the ground. Bodices were fitted and often low-backed or halter-necked. Such gowns played a dual role as they could be dressed up with fashionable boleros and tiny bed jackets and worn for intimate dinners within the house.

During the 1950s, gowns were full length, bed jackets shrank to bolero size with narrow collars, and elbow length sleeves became particularly popular, whether bell shaped or gathered into a high puff, especially when teamed with yoked negligees which swirled out from masses of tiny gathers to reach the knee.

Cotton, terylene blends, georgette silks, wool mixes, crepes and chiffon were popular fabrics of the 1960s. Long, square necked nightdresses were eclipsed by 'baby dolls', little cotton 'short-suits' which were lightly frilled or ruffled. Fabrics were decorative, with spots, broderie anglaise or prints, and were adorned with ribbons and bows.

By the following decade, frilly baby dolls had disappeared to be supplanted by long, soft jersey or chiffon nightdresses which could be plain or printed. Many women discarded nightwear altogether, whilst others adopted the unisex look and favoured pyjamas. Now, anything goes, with cotton or jersey shirts, silk camisoles, french knickers, petticoats and cami-knickers all worn as nightwear.

▶ **Janet Reger:** nightdress and robe made from chiffon trimmed with lace.

▲ **Laetitia Allen:** chemise.

▼ **Laetitia Allen:** 'English Rose' vest and shorts.

◀ **Jane Woolrich:** Bias-cut and panelled nightdress in silk satin and co-ordinating deep dyed leavers lace. The deep plunging back has criss cross detail.

▲ **De Pledge:** 'Opulence' nightdress and jacket in pure silk with delicate trim.

▼ **Hanro of Switzerland:** 'Fashion Seduction' silk nightdress and negligee with narrow silk satin trim and pearl button fastenings.

▶ **Hanro of Switzerland:** nightdress and negligee.

◀ **Rose Lewis:** negligee.

▲ **La Senza:** 2-piece suit in spot
cotton jersey.

▼ **Janet Reger:** 'Alex' pyjama in tailored
silk satin.

▼ **Janet Reger:** 'Nadja' nightdress and robe in
pure silk satin and chiffon, appliqued with
sumptuous French lace.

▼ **Hanro of Switzerland:** pyjamas.

▲ **Hanro of Switzerland:** nightdress
and negligee.

Panties

At the beginning of the nineteenth century, panties, or drawers, consisted of two tubes of fabric cut wide and full and gathered into a waistband. Left open at the crotch and with ties at the front, they were made from cotton, fine lawn, crepe de Chine or silk but were not commonly worn by women until the 1840s.

Forty years later, drawers were closed at the crotch, though they were still full and wide. When gathered to the knee, they were known as 'knickerbockers' or 'knickerbocker drawers', though such styles were not popular with all women, particularly older women, who continued to wear the open crotch drawers.

After the First World War, knickerbockers gained a button inbetween and became increasingly short to match rising skirt lengths. The 1920s and 1930s saw the appearance of wide French knickers and cami-knickers, the latter being a combination of the chemise or camisole and drawers, basically a princess petticoat joined between the legs with a gusset or flap. Most were cut with a full leg, the length of which varied from hip to mid-thigh, and were made in a variety of colours and materials: cotton, muslin, silk, lawn or crepe de Chine.

Knickers and cami-knickers became increasingly shorter until, in the 1930s, they became known as 'pants' or 'panties'. Underwear, like other items of clothing, was affected by rationing in the Second World War, but vests and knickers from this period were of a high quality, even if they were cut economically, whilst the same could not be said of corsets and stockings.

Panties remained modest in cut during the 1950s and 1960s, and it was not until the 1970s and 1980s, as panties became briefs and bikini styles grew in popularity, that 'flesh' was revealed. As fashionable clothes became tighter and more clinging, panties had to be gathered at the hip rather than the waist and designs attempted to minimize 'VPL' (visible pantie line). Cami-knickers were revived in the 1980s in a variety of fabrics, and with the prevalence of elastane fibres in lingerie manufacture, controlling stomach panels in both high cut and low cut styles can provide light support for all figures.

▶ **Triumph International:** 'Bijou brief' with 35 per cent Lycra elastane. Fabric, cut and seaming combine to flatten the tummy and lift the behind, creating a perfect figure.

Hanro of Switzerland

▶ **Hanro of Switzerland:**
high cut brief.

▲ **Hanro of Switzerland:** low cut brief.

Panties

▲ **Knickerbox:** underwired bra and matching flared shorts in classic ivory antique 1940s-styled silk with side button fastening.

▶ **Knickerbox:** 'Exquisite Rose Lace Collection' high cut brief and underwired bra set.

 ◀ **Silhouette:** 'Audace' thong and bra.
▼

▶ **Silhouette:** 'Baroque' thong brief and balconette bra set.

▼ **Playtex:** 'Superlook Secrets'
control brief. Two pieces of fabric
are fused in the tummy panel giving
support where it's needed.

▲ **Playtex:** 'Superlook Secrets' high
cut brief in satin.

◄ **La Perla:** 'Maison'.

▼ **Malizia by La Perla:** 'Pin Up'.

▲ **Knickerbox:** 'Forfit' double faced vest and hot pants.

▼ **Playtex:** 'Cherish' control high cut
brief with stretch lace trim and
controlling front panel.

Hanro of Switzerland

▼ **Hanro of Switzerland:** high cut brief and bra set.

▲ **Hanro of Switzerland:**
medium cut brief.

▲ **Sloggi:** 'Sloggi 200' string.

◀ **Triumph International:** 'Jessica' string brief in printed charmeuse combined with scalloped lace.

▶ **Sloggi:** 'Sloggi' Maxi brief. The core-spun cotton with Lycra elastane fabric's 2-way stretch ensures a perfect fit.

▼ **Lovable:** 'Lov'Up' control brief with centre seam, up-lift panels in shiny Lycra satinette and lace detailing across the tummy to disguise the control panel.

▼ **Lovable Italiana:** seamless
underwired bra and brief in cotton,
polymide and elastane.

▶ **Warners:** Lace with Lycra peach bra under C&B London maroon Lace with Lycra tiny T-shirt; French Jenny black and white 'flocked' rose Lace with Lycra 1950s knickers.

▲ **Janet Reger:** underwired bra and hot pant in intricate two-tone lace.

▼ **Patricia of Finland**

▲ **Damart:** boxer pants.

Petticoats and slips

The term 'petticoat' originally referred to a visible layer of the skirt, but by the late sixteenth century petticoats were worn as woollen underskirts, principally to provide warmth. Over subsequent centuries, petticoats have been stretched over farthingales, have stiffened skirts and, when revealed at the hem, were embellished with lace or embroidery.

In the early twentieth century silk was the principal fabric used in petticoats, and the development of fast dyeing methods saw an increase in the use of vibrant colours and printed decoration. The slim line and bias cutting of 1920s' outerwear demanded simple full-length slips cut on the cross.

The Utility designs of the 1940s meant that the petticoat was cut very straight, without design details such as pleats, in order to save on fabric. The understandable increase in the amount of fabric used by the 1950s led to full-length circular skirts which required generous layers of petticoats. The decade also saw the large-scale manufacture of man made fabrics such as nylon. Nylon had been invented in 1938 but could not be fully developed for commercial use until after the Second World War. With cotton and, especially, silk still expensive after the restrictions of wartime, nylon was hailed for its easycare properties: it could be washed easily, did not need to be ironed, was non-absorbent but also could also be woven to be porous. It was the dominant material for the next two decades.

The waist slip rose up high to follow the popular mini-skirt in the 1960s and came back down again to accommodate the full-length skirts of the 1970s. The end of the latter decade and revival of glamour in the 1980s saw silk petticoats returning to favour, though a continuing and major concern has been to develop a cling-resistant, anti-static man made fabric, with fabric mixes combining artificial fibres such as nylon and polyester with cotton or Lycra.

La Senza: 'Body Sculptures' bra and hip slip with in built panty.

▼ **Embodiment:** 'Fifi' knee-length
side split slip finished with double-
edged lace and net trim.

◀ **Janet Reger:** bra slip in pure silk and satin, appliqued with sumptuous French lace and with in-built padded and wired bra.

▼ **Janet Reger:** mini slip in pure silk satin with lace trim.

Index

Allen, Laetitia 20, 58, 59

backless bras 22
balconette bras 14-5, 28
bodies 46, 51, 52, 53, 54, 55, 56, 64, 65, 67
bras 10-45
broderie anglais 18, 36
bustier 15, 29, 36

C&B London 60
Cacherel 35
Calais lace 15, 54
cami top 10, 58
cami-knickers 46, 96
camisoles 46, 50
chemise 46, 84
chiffon 25, 63, 83
combinations 46
corsets 9, 68-81
cropped tops 9, 46, 57
cup design 10

Damart 42, 62, 63, 80, 81, 62, 63, 119
De Pledge 78, 87

Eda 24-5, 61
elastic 68

elastomeric fibres 9
Embodiment 122
embroidery 32, 36, 47, 86
Exotica: Knickers from Brazil 89
Exquisite Form 40

fabric manufacture 9
Felina 41
Fila Donna 45
fitting 10, 40, 68
French knickers 50

Gaultier 9
girdles 71
Gossard 8-9, 34, 72, 73
Gottex 12, 13, 54, 55

Hanro of Switzerland 46, 47, 56, 57, 88, 89, 94, 95, 98, 99, 110, 111
health 68

jersey 10, 18

Karan, Donna 16
knickerbockers 96
Knickerbox 100, 101, 108

La Perla 9-10, 26, 27, 65, 77, 106
La Senza 21, 38, 66, 91

▼ **Gossard:** 'Ritz' in blueberry.

Index

lace 6, 12, 27, 37, 76, 78

Lace with Lycra 16, 17, 34, 35,
    60, 117

Lejaby 18-19

Lewis, Rose 90

liberty bodice 46

Lovable Italiana 32, 33, 114, 115

Lycra 9, 10, 29, 43, 55

Madonna 9

Malizia by La Perla 64, 107

microfibres 18

negligee 82

nightwear 46, 82-95

nylon 68, 120

outerwear 9, 46

panties 96-119

Patricia of Finland 43, 79, 118

petticoats 120

Playtex 2-3, 104, 105, 109

pyjamas 92, 94

racer back 42, 45

Reger, Janet 6-7, 82-3, 92, 93,
    116, 122

Rigby & Peller 48-9, 68, 69

Rosy 17

Silhouette 22, 23, 52, 53, 70,
    74, 75, 102, 103

sizing 10

slips 6, 120-23

Sloggi 112, 113

sports bras 42, 43, 44

stretch fabrics 9, 10, 12

Summers, Ann 71

Swiss embroidery 15, 29, 64

tanga 59, 112

thongs 37, 48, 53

Triumph International 44, 96-7

underwiring 12, 20, 21, 33, 39,
    49, 100, 101

Valisere 36, 50, 51

vests 46, 57, 60, 62, 63, 85

VPL 96

Warners 14-15, 28, 29, 67, 117

Wolfords 60

Woolrich, Jane 36, 76-7, 86

▶ **Lovable Italiana:** 'Scintille'
underwired bra and deep brief.